Betrayed *into* Purpose

SHERIDA HUGHEY

ISBN 979-8-88540-435-8 (paperback)
ISBN 979-8-88540-436-5 (digital)

Copyright © 2022 by Sherida Hughey

All rights reserved. No part of this publication may be reproduced, distributed, or transmitted in any form or by any means, including photocopying, recording, or other electronic or mechanical methods without the prior written permission of the publisher. For permission requests, solicit the publisher via the address below.

Christian Faith Publishing
832 Park Avenue
Meadville, PA 16335
www.christianfaithpublishing.com

Printed in the United States of America

Have you ever felt like each day you wake up is just another day? Just existing and wondering how to live? Just going through the motions of whatever comes with each new day?

This is the place Diamond once was in this thing called life. We only get one, and it is up to no one else but you to make the best of it! Along the way, God allows people to be either a blessing or a lesson, sometimes both. Not everyone that enters our lives is meant to be there for a lifetime. Most people are there for a season, and it is very imperative to be able to discern when their time in your life expires.

Diamond was at a crossroad in her life and had looked out for those who were near and dear to her heart and just wanted someone to have her back for a change. Her king was not going to fall out of the sky, so it was time for her to get off of her throne so that her king could find his queen.

A Night Out on the Town

It was springtime in the early '90s, one Friday night. Diamond needed to get out on the town and get her groove on. Dancing is one thing that allowed her to feel free. Diamond and her cousin Tasha ended up at a hole in the wall on the southside of Memphis, Tennessee. Diamond, a California girl, usually stood out most of the time she decided to get out as that was not as often as it should have been. But there was something unique about Diamond. She was not the typical hood rat. She had class and an aura about herself that was very intriguing.

After a night of dancing and getting their drink on, Diamond and Tasha sat at the bar until Tasha returned to the dance floor. Diamond was not interested in any of the men that had approached her up to that point and decided to order some hot wings and chill. Tasha, being Tasha, was trying to find her a "D" for the night! They were like sisters, although blood-related cousins, and Diamond never judged her for enjoying one-night stands.

Diamond, on the other hand, was more of a relationship type that had been with her high school sweetheart for the past six years but had recently broken things off with him. Diamond was not the clubbing type but just needed to get out and dance, which is why she found herself at the Hole in the Wall! Otherwise, she would be spending another Friday night at home doing NOTHING!

Diamond was going in on those hot wings and was so unbothered by the guys that tried to get attention. Meanwhile, Tasha had found her "D" for the night—and cute, might I add! Little did he know he was about to get beat out of his "D"!

Tasha and Lamar returned from the dance floor, both sexually stimulated, and were ready to leave the Hole in the Wall! Lamar called his cousin Percy over to the bar, attempting to play matchmaker. Diamond spoke to Percy and kept going in on her hot wings! Percy was not Diamond's type, but a little conversation never hurt anybody. She had crossed paths with her future husband.

Percy was a tall, light-skinned, semi-muscular with a receding hairline, and very handsome dude. He and Diamond engaged in small talk as did Tasha and Lamar. It was getting late, and the Hole in the Wall would be soon closing. They decided to continue getting to know each other outside in the parking lot.

Tasha and Lamar left together, and after a long debate, Diamond agreed to drop Percy off at home, not something that she was accustomed to, so she made sure her knife was within reach, just in case Percy tried something. He seemed harmless, was very handsome, and very comical, which made the fifteen-minute ride an enjoyable one.

Shortly after they left the Hole in the Wall, they arrived at Percy's mom's home. They exchanged phone numbers, said their goodbyes, and Diamond sped off, heading back to the northside of Memphis.

About thirty minutes later, Percy called her to make sure she made it home safely. They talked briefly as Percy packed his duffel bag, preparing to go out of town for work in the next few hours. Diamond asked Percy to give her a call when he got back in town, and they would go from there. She was sure she wanted to get to know him better and see where it went. "Well, I guess I'm going to call it a night, Percy. It's been nice meeting and talking to you! See you when you get back in town! Good night!"

Diamond climbed in bed, closed her eyes, and started drifting off to sleep until she heard a knock at the door. "Who is it?" she asked with irritation in her voice.

"Tasha!"

Diamond opened the door, and there stood Tasha and Lamar, all hugged up as if they had known each other for years. Diamond was not the least bit surprised. She just returned to her bed as Tasha and Lamar did a beeline to Diamond's guest bedroom.

Know When It's Over

A couple weeks had passed, and Percy just returned home.

"Hello, Diamond speaking!"

"Hey, what's up, girl? Did you miss me?"

"Tell me who is calling, and I'll let you know if I missed you!"

"Damn, shorty, it's like that?" He laughed.

"Hey, Percy, how are you doing? I was just kidding. Of course, I missed you, a little!"

"So when can I see you, shorty?"

"You can come by tomorrow or Thursday, after I go to the grocery store. Do you like meatloaf? I'll cook us some dinner."

"Hell, yeah. Okay, what time?"

"I'm not sure, but I'll be in touch. I can't talk right now. I'm helping my little sister with her homework. Can I give you a call when I get them to bed later or tomorrow?"

"Okay, cool. So they live with you?"

"Yes, I have had legal custody of them since my eighteenth birthday. I'm twenty-one now!"

"Much respect to you, shorty. Okay, I'll see you soon. Good night!"

"Ashley, you ready for me to check your homework?"

"Yes, I just finished my spelling words. I'm ready for you to test me!"

"Okay, be there in just a minute! Dominique, have you finished taking your bath yet? And clean out the bathtub when you are done. Run Ashley some bathwater, please!"

"Okay!"

"And get ready for bed, Dominique. Good night."

There was a knock at the door.

"Who is it?"

"Eric, baby. Can we talk, please? I love you."

"Talk about what? I told you it's over!"

"Baby, please let me in!"

"No! And stop showing up here unannounced! I'm getting ready for bed. Leave before I call the police! And don't come back. I have moved on, and you should too!"

"I'll leave for now, but we need to talk. Call me when you get a chance tomorrow, or can I come by when the girls go to school in the morning?"

"NO! We don't have anything to talk about. Your ass is psycho! I'm dating someone else now!"

"What?"

"Yeah. Now leave me the hell alone! I'm calling the police. This conversation is over! Ashley, come out of the bathroom and get ready for bed!"

The phone rang, and Diamond answered, "Hello, Diamond speaking!"

"Hey, what's up, shorty?"

"Hey, Percy, what's up with you?"

"Are you cooking dinner tonight? Is it cool for me to come through?"

"Okay, bet!"

"I'll be over around 6:30 or 7:00!"

"Okay, see you then!"

*****

"Dominique! Ashley! It's time to get up and get ready for school. Hurry up, girls. I overslept and didn't hear the alarm sound off! We're running late, hurry up! I won't have time to stop by McDonald's, so I'll put some Pop-Tarts in the toaster. Come on, Ashley, let me make you a ponytail while Dominique is in the bathroom, then you can go get your Pop-Tart. Dominique, come on out of the bathroom so

I can make you a ponytail. We need to get out of here! I'm going to the grocery store after school. I have invited a friend over for dinner tonight."

"Okay," they both answered at the same time.

"Have a good day at school and be good!"

Diamond could not get back home fast enough! She was exhausted from lack of rest. She had not been getting much sleep since she broke up with Eric. He repeatedly called the phone and stopped by her place randomly. Sometimes he just sat outside and watched outside of her apartment to see if she would have any male visitors.

As soon as Diamond made it back home, the phone rang. "Hello, Diamond speaking!"

"Good morning, baby, can I come over now?"

"Hell no, Eric, and why are you still calling my damn phone? I see now I need to get a restraining order. Why can't you just leave me the hell alone? Damn!" Diamond slammed the phone down. "The only way I'm going to get some rest is to take this phone off the hook!"

Getting Acquainted

There was a knock at the door.

"Who is it?"

"It's Percy, shorty!"

"Okay, coming! Hey, Percy! Hey, what's up, Lamar?"

"What's up, Diamond?"

"What's up, shorty. I thought I was at the wrong door! Some dude was just peeping in your window when we pulled up, then he got in a white car and pulled off but kept looking back trying to see which door we were about to knock on! You better be careful. Is that your ex you were telling me about? I hope that fool don't run up on me. I don't want to beat dude's ass! You might need to go on and get that paperwork done at MPD for real. His ass is crazy!"

"I told you! I'm so tired of his stupid ass! Maybe he will go on about his business now that he's seen your big Amazon ass!" They laughed. "Will you be my bodyguard?" Diamond laughed some more. "Come on in and make yourselves at home. I'm almost finished cooking. Just waiting on the cornbread, and we can eat. Would y'all like something to drink? I don't have any liquor, just sweet tea, water, or Kool-Aid."

"It's all good, shorty. Lamar did a BYOB. Have some Remy?"

"No, I'm good! I don't drink during the week and especially not with Eric's stupid ass driving by. I need to be alert at all times, just in case I have to regulate on that fool!"

"Dominique! Ashley! Get ready for dinner!"

"Okay!"

"Percy and Lamar, we will eat in the living room. I want to watch *In Living Color*. I love that show!" They all laughed.

"Diamond, can I have some Kool-Aid?"

"Eat some of your food, Ashley!"

"And may I have another piece of meatloaf and cornbread, please?"

"Yes, eat some of your cabbage too!"

"Okay!"

"Man, shorty, dinner was good as hell. Thanks for the invite! I could get used to eating this home cooking every day! Well, it's getting late, and I know you have to get the girls ready for bed, and you have to go to work tomorrow, so we'll go on and bounce. I'll hit you up when I make it to the crib!"

"Nice seeing you again, Lamar. Hope you enjoyed dinner too!"

"Hell, yeah, Diamond. Thanks! Oh! And tell your cousin she didn't have to beat me out of my meat like that!" He laughed.

"What? So you haven't talked to her since that night?"

"No. Every time I call, her kids' father is there!"

"Oh, well, he does live there. She didn't tell you that?"

"Hell, no, but it's all good though!"

"Well, be safe out there!"

The phone rang.

"Hello, Diamond speaking!"

"Hey, what's up, cousin?"

"Hey, girl, what's up with you?"

"Girl, nothing. Bored as hell, and these kids getting on my damn nerves!" She laughed.

"Girl, guess who just left from over my house?"

"Who, bitch?"

"Percy and Lamar, girl!"

"Oh, damn. Why are they over there? And why you didn't call me?"

"Well, it was kind of last minute. I invited them over for dinner."

"Oh, okay. So it's like that!"

"Girl, whatever. I wanted to see Percy, and Lamar brought him over here. And Lamar said you didn't have to beat him out of his meat like that!" She laughed.

"Girl, he is fine as hell. But that meat wasn't all that! Hell, I got six kids. I have been busy as hell! Anyway, have you given it up to Percy yet?"

"Hell, no, girl. You know I don't give it up that easy! If we hook up again, I might. But his 'D' print is big as hell, so I'm kind of scared to give him some unless we start dating!" (Ladies, one thing you don't do is tell another woman the size of your man's love muscle or how good he is in bed. NEVER! ABSOLUTELY NOT!)

I Am My Sisters' Keeper

As time went on, Diamond and Percy started seeing each other on a regular basis. Diamond met all the homies and Percy's immediate family. It was official. They were a couple. They were partying on a regular basis, so Diamond chose to separate her partying lifestyle from raising her sisters, so she decided to give their mom, Honey, an opportunity to reconnect with her daughters.

Dominique and Ashley began spending weekends with Honey since she was in a stable environment. Honey was not clean, but she was in her own place and not on the streets anymore. They continued to spend summer vacations and holidays with their dad, Paul, as usual.

Honey had been in and out of the girls' lives most of their lives due to her drug addiction. Her addiction caused her family to relocate from California to Memphis, destroying the two-parent home forever. Diamond was at the point in her life that she wanted less responsibility since she felt robbed of her adolescence. Being an older sister, she wanted to protect her sisters and make sure they never ended up in foster care, separated from her family. She had been caring for her sisters since age thirteen with the help of their father, Paul, Grandmother, Ms. Clara, and their Aunt Martha.

Diamond never resented her sisters. It was as if she knew deep down in her heart that God had given her the assignment of watching over them, and she never questioned it. She gladly took on the responsibility, but it was time for someone to look out for Diamond for a change, hold her down, be what she was to everyone that crossed her path, a blessing. Would Percy be the man that God created just for Diamond? Or would he be someone placed in her life for a season, serving his purpose in Diamond's life? Only time would tell!

Dominique and Ashley loved their mom, Honey, and wanted to spend more and more time with her in hopes of making up for lost time. Honey also loved her girls, but her drug addiction was very difficult to overcome. Many times, she checked herself into rehabs with hopes of beating her addiction so that she could salvage her relationship with her children.

Honey's son, Damon, wanted nothing to do with her as he blamed her for losing an athletic scholarship to college. He also blamed her for the life of poverty that they lived once they made it to Memphis. He resented her drug use because it divided their family and put a wedge between them and the only father figure that he had known and loved so dearly, the man that taught him all about sports, and the man that raised him as his own son from ages two to fifteen. Honey and Paul's breakup happened at a very critical time in Diamond and Damon's lives, from living the California dream to a Memphis nightmare.

Diamond was ready to explore life with Percy and see where it took them. She was looking for an escape into a more positive direction, but God had other intentions. Sometimes God has to break us in order to fix us!

Diamond was in deep with her now live-in boyfriend, Percy. He was no longer traveling, making his living in construction. Percy decided he wanted to dance with the devil by becoming a street pharmacist making fast money. Diamond, at times, found herself making drops here and there part-time while she worked as medical receptionist in the medical center, which was only minutes from her best clients.

Because of the change of events in Diamond's lifestyle, she thought it was best that Dominique and Ashley went to live with their mom. Honey was not clean, but she did have shelter for the girls. Diamond and Percy didn't provide a kid-friendly environment for the girls to live with them as they were married and full-blown street pharmacists. They were selling drugs out of their home, which was not the best environment for preteen girls.

Throw a Whole Decade Away

Diamond and Percy were living the fast life. They were partying almost every night, waking up getting high, and going to bed high. Diamond had transformed into a street-smart businesswoman that was very intelligent yet still made unwise choices in her life. Diamond decided to walk away from her legit income and become a full-time hustler.

Although they made lots of money, they blew every dime as soon as they made it because they knew they could make it right back. Years had passed, and Diamond became bored with the fast life, partying and hanging out with her street family, which included Percy's cousins, childhood friends and associates that were also street pharmacists. Diamond was the responsible one of the pair, making sure the bills were paid while Percy splurged on whatever he wanted.

Diamond felt the distance that became evident between them and grew suspicious. Percy's pager persistently sounded off. At first, she didn't think much about it since he was a street pharmacist. However, things just were not adding up. Percy was always away from home yet had nothing to show for his absence. She was sure that he was cheating again and started hearing rumors that Percy was getting high off of his own supply! Although he never smoked anything besides weed in Diamond's presence, she was questioned by some of Percy's family whether he was lacing his blunts with cocaine.

As time continued, Percy's cheating and lack of growth irritated Diamond so much so that she began seeking the attention of other men. It was not the lack of attention from Percy that bothered Diamond. It was the lack of financial support that provoked her to start spending time with other men, seeking financial support. She couldn't care less about the trifling actions of Percy. He could do whatever he wanted in the streets at that point because she was no longer interested in sex with him. It was the lack of financial support that she could not deal with any longer.

Enough is enough, she thought, so she decided to move out of their dwelling and moved in with an associate that they both knew, which turned out to be Percy's cousin Keisha. Diamond was fed up with footing the bills, and since Percy would not leave, she thought it would be best that she left. What was the point? Six years in a relationship with a man that did not want to build a life of stability but just wanted to get by with little to no contribution. What was the point?

The roommate situation was a good idea, so Diamond thought. But Keisha had her own demons she was dealing with which included a cocaine habit that Diamond accidentally discovered. Keisha was not paying the bills that Diamond gave her half on, and that roommate situation ended a couple of months later.

Diamond had no choice but to move back home with Percy. She agreed to go back home only if they could move into another dwelling. She could not take a chance of living there and not knowing if Percy entertained his THOTS there.

Diamond slipped into a very depressed state. What had she been doing almost a decade of her life?

This Too Shall Pass

Time quickly elapsed. Diamond and Percy continued to coexist in the same dwelling, squandering precious time, accomplishing close to nothing as a unit. Diamond experienced such a void in her life and in her spirit. She desired for Percy to feel the emptiness that consumed her, so she leaped on the "cheating bus!" Although she knew two wrongs would never make it right, she had a hidden agenda for each man that she devoured. They unknowingly had to pay for the pain Percy was causing her.

Diamond used the gift of gab to persuade men to do whatever she desired them to do. She gave them false hope, knowing good and damn well she wanted nothing more than to be sexually gratified and financially compensated. One after another, she pierced hearts and never gave it a second thought.

Trust was nonexistent. They both were cheating, and Percy had become mentally and physically abusive. Diamond refused to be another domestic violence statistic or DV story on the news, so she knew something had to be done. Diamond was preparing for a way of escape, but Percy had such a hold on her. She loved him like she had never loved any other man in her life. For the last two years of their marriage, Diamond evolved into a woman with a prayer and a plan.

Diamond's disappointment sickened her. What had she been doing an entire decade of her life? For the sake of their wedding vows, would she stay with a man that never acknowledged God, cheated, did not provide for her, and degraded her every opportunity he had? If she was going to accomplish anything positive in her life, she would have to remove the deadweight that was weighing her down. Just going through the motions, the coexisting continued.

Although she was fed up with his abusive actions, she knew the marriage would be just another chapter in her life that would soon come to an end. Deep down inside, she knew she deserved so much more than what she received from Percy. He had done a number on her. With very little self-esteem and a lot of self-doubt, Diamond was stuck in that dead-end rut a couple more years. Needless to say, the next two years would be the most productive and meaningful two years of her life.

Let's Do This

The cheating rumors kept surfacing, but Diamond stayed focused. There were even rumors around town that Percy and Tasha had hooked up during one of Percy and Diamond's many separations. When confronted, they both denied the allegations. However, Percy told Diamond that Tasha came on to him, which was unquestionable given her track record of being a whore.

The sisterhood between Diamond and Tasha would be destroyed forever. Deep down inside, Diamond's gut could not believe them. Maybe they did not hook up, but that truth would never be discovered.

Percy, on the other hand, totally untrustworthy, would never make love to his beloved wife willingly again. He only received sexual gratification from her if he forced himself into her. We refer to this as rape, but how can a man rape his own wife?

Diamond continued her own rendezvous with male friends that also desired her physically. She surrounded herself with more positive people that wanted her to succeed in life. She formed a great friendship with Chris, Lamar's roommate, who was in their circle of friends. Chris hated the way Percy treated Diamond and reassured her that she was worthy of being treated like royalty.

The more time Chris and Diamond hung out together outside of their circle of friends, the more they realized they had so much in common. And by coincidence, they shared the same birthday. True friendship was what Diamond needed to help her regain her dignity and boost her self-esteem. They talked and laughed for hours at a time, which would be the best therapy that any psychologist could offer and better than any medicine.

Their bond grew deeper and deeper with each episode of philosophical conversations. Diamond never even had that type of bond with Percy. With Chris, she could be as deep or silly as she wanted without judgment of any type. Diamond could even share her dreams and aspirations with Chris. He was very encouraging as any good friend is expected to be. If Diamond had a smile on her face and felt good about herself, nothing else seemed to matter.

Their friendship was never about sex. In fact, Chris had been in their circle of friends about five years, but he always had respect for Percy and Diamond's union. They only became intimately involved once Diamond reassured Chris that she would divorce Percy and that she wanted so much so to be freed from the bondage that came along with their union.

Their sexual escapades only took place when Diamond desired sexual gratification. Diamond had never experienced multiple orgasms with Percy, which did not surprise her. Chris loved her unconditionally, and she felt it so deeply, which she never experienced that type of unconditional love from any man until they crossed paths. For once in her life, Diamond realized what it was like to have a soul mate.

When a Woman Is Fed Up

Antwon, another male friend of Diamond's, also voiced his disgust of the way Percy treated Diamond. Antwon was best friends with one of Percy's younger cousins. Antwon and Diamond often escaped the circle of friends they had in common to experience life away from their usual grind spot. Antwon and Diamond enjoyed getting money together. In fact, the way Diamond hustled like a dude was what caught Antwon's attention. Diamond, at that point, was tired of Percy and just wanted him to leave. She was getting the attention of a younger man that also expressed to Diamond that she deserved to be genuinely loved by a real man.

At that point, they were only friends that enjoyed each other's company. They had not been intimate, although rumors started to spread. Diamond would often drive up to their grind spot and toot her car horn for Antwon to ride out with her. They both enjoyed shopping, so they often got away to a shopping mall, lunch dates, trips to the local casinos, or just drove to the riverfront for a nice stroll.

Although Antwon wanted Diamond badly, he never once pressured her for sex. Her companionship was plenty for him, and besides, Antwon knew Diamond was worth waiting for. Although it looked very suspicious of them both leaving the grind spot together, Antwon was very harmless. The word would often get back to Percy that his wife came by to pick Antwon up, and Percy once again felt the betrayal he had made Diamond feel for years. Percy even confronted Antwon, questioning whether he was sleeping with Diamond. Their friendship would continue for years to come. Diamond eventually gave Antwon the "business!"

Goodbye, Nightlife

Percy and Diamond's party life continued. However, the circle of friends started drifting apart. When they all hit the club scene, they were about twenty deep male and females—Percy/Diamond, Lamar/Michelle, "C-Note"/Tonya, Barry, Antwon, Larry, Chris, Keisha, Tasha, and a few others. They would often go to the Hole in the Wall on the southside of Memphis. They would enter the club as an entourage of neighborhood superstars!

Everyone had their own individual 750 ml of their favorite alcoholic beverage. Diamond's drink of choice was Alizé/Hennessey, and they smoked out the entire back of the club with no less than a half-pound of weed, more than likely a bit more. This would be the last group outing Diamond participated in. She and Percy were headed toward a divorce, and she was tired of "fronting" like she was content in her marriage to Percy.

Diamond was determined that she would not keep just existing, but she was ready to live a life of purpose. She began soul-searching and started attending church. A few visits later, Diamond decided to join. Her hustling shifted from drugs to a somewhat legal hustle, colored contact lens. She had a hookup on bulk and began to resell them at four times her cost per pair. She developed wiser spending habits.

Diamond also continued handling her responsibilities, shelter, and transportation. Then Diamond decided to enroll in a local technology school to become a certified nail technician. Classes would begin in the fall. For the first time in a long while, she had established some short-term goals and was looking forward to her life without Percy.

Percy continued his own shenanigans, but Diamond was so unconcerned with how he was spending his time. She was on a mission. She did not attend church every Sunday, but she attended more often than she once did, which was only on holidays. The more she attended, the less hopeless she felt. Life finally began to have more meaning!

Hurt People Hurt People

The next year would be a challenge. Although the nail tech course only took nine months to complete, Diamond knew it would not be a walk in the park. It was as if Satan knew when she was about to make positive changes in her life. He threw every type of obstacle imaginable in Diamond's direction.

Percy's verbal abuse turned more physical, resulting in several domestic violence police reports filed, resulting in an Order of Protection. She also armed herself with a handgun, which she was not afraid to use. In fact, she had even shot at Percy several times, just barely missing him. She was close to reaching her breaking point. Everyone has one.

The more they drifted apart, the closer she drifted toward God. Diamond yearned for a deeper relationship with God and would not allow anyone to interfere with that, not even Percy. Diamond still loved Percy despite his trifling ways and wanted him also to experience a relationship with God. She even convinced him to accompany her to church a few times, hoping he would be transformed into a God-fearing man. Percy would often say, "I don't want to waste the preacher's time since I'm going to hell anyway!" Who says that, right?

Diamond enjoyed how she felt when she left church on Sunday afternoon and wanted Percy to experience that same joy, then maybe he would stop the abuse. The idea of her husband attending church by her side on a regular basis was not her reality. The thought of her attending church without him made him furious. He often accused Diamond of cheating on him with men at her church, which was a result of his own guilt.

The more active she became in church, the more frequent the accusations occurred. She spent less time with her street friends and more time with her new church family. She did join the crew now and then. However, she felt out of place. She was transitioning to Christianity and just did not feel right occasionally smoking weed, drinking, and partying with the crew anymore. Diamond's transformation became so apparent that Michelle, Lamar's girlfriend, even started calling Diamond "choir girl." It did not even faze Diamond because she was on a mission and was seeing positive results.

Most Saturdays, Diamond was content staying home and not going out to party. One Saturday night in particular, Percy came home from a night of drinking and partying, only to find Diamond peacefully sleeping, and decided to awaken her with more cheating accusations. Percy pulled Diamond out of bed in a rage, tore her clothes off, then threw her back on the bed, and forced himself on top of her as she struggled to get away from him. He had gotten fed up with Diamond's constant rejection.

She had not had sex with Percy in months, and he was sure she was getting sexual gratification elsewhere. He began choking her to the point that she was almost lifeless. He stopped choking her once she had gotten too tired to continue fighting him off. She just laid there as he penetrated her unwilling dry vagina until he climaxed. She cried the entire time, thinking, *Now I know why rape victims feel violated!*

Percy passed out right on top of her, and Diamond managed to get from underneath him. Percy was a big man. He was about six-foot-five, three hundred pounds, and was muscular in build. She went straight to the bathroom to clean herself up. She caught a glimpse of her red inflamed neck with Percy's handprint embedded around her neck. Diamond fell to the floor, crying, and asked God why He was allowing her to go through such a terrible situation. What had she done to deserve such treatment from a man that vowed to love, cherish, and honor her until death?

The thought of getting her gun and blowing Percy's head off crossed her mind. Lawfully, it may have been justified since she had filed several police reports regarding domestic violence, including having a valid Order of Protection. Then she realized if she killed him, that scene would replay in her head for the rest of her life, and she could not live with that constant reminder. Her thought then shifted to ending her own life. She had attempted overdosing unsuccessfully twice, failing both times. She did not know how much more pain she would be able to endure from Percy. Her mind was all over the place.

After soaking in a hot Epsom salt bath for hours, imagining herself killing Percy, she got out the tub and dried herself off. She put on a pair of sweats and an oversized T-shirt, although it was the middle of the summer, but her body felt unimaginably cold to the point that she was shivering. She removed her .380 automatic handgun from her closet shelf, which she kept loaded and stood right over Percy's drunken passed-out body. Diamond could have taken his life in that moment, but a small still voice said, "NO!" Diamond contemplated suicide, putting the gun to her own temple but just could not pull the trigger.

Diamond put the gun back on the shelf and fell to her knees, crying out to God, "Lord, please take the pain away!" She continued to pray to God, again questioning Him as to why He was allowing her to go through the hell she was experiencing. Little did Diamond know God was shifting her into her purpose!

Faith without Works Is Dead

Diamond grew more and more into isolation. She needed to understand what was occurring in her life and why Percy would not leave. Whenever she was not studying her nail technology books, she was studying her Bible. Being productive gave her peace of mind and motivated Diamond to prepare to walk away from the facade that some may refer to as a happy marriage. She remained optimistic despite the negative comments and constant belittling by Percy. Furthermore, she was determined to be happy.

Diamond was determined to perfect her newly discovered passion for nail care services. Once she learned the basics, about six months into her course, it was going down! She began offering manicures to her family and associates while practicing and perfecting her craft. She offered $5 manicures to her cousin Rodney and all of his friends while building a clientele. Diamond carried her nail kit with her everywhere she went, occupying her time in a productive way while securing a successful career in the beauty industry.

Diamond continued selling contact lens. However, her hustle was not as booming as it once was, but she maintained her bills and paid the tuition. She held her own as time continued to progress with only a couple months until graduation. She was well on her way to creating a life that brought her joy! Percy continued being in the streets, but Diamond was so unbothered with whatever he had going on. She was only concerned with her future. As far as she was concerned, that marriage was over, and she was preparing for the next chapters of her life!

The more Diamond read her Bible and surrounded herself with positive people that encouraged her, such as Antwon and Chris, the more peace she found. Paula, Percy's sister, was also encouraging Diamond to do what was best for her. Although Paula loved her brother, she knew their marriage was too toxic to salvage. At that point, there was absolutely no trust. They were both cheating, and sooner or later, they would probably kill each other or Diamond would snap and kill Percy!

Diamond discovered a new hobby at the local casinos, blackjack! Although she was trying to figure out what Christianity was all about, she needed an outlet to pass the time until she was free from the bondage of her unhealthy marriage. Diamond once again stumbled upon yet another hustle to compensate for Percy's lack of financial support. She mastered the game of blackjack in a short period of time. She was not sure if she was experiencing beginner's luck or if someone was cutting those cards on her behalf, but she was WINNING! Her hustle money was making her more money, and she no longer relied on being a street pharmacist!

Weeks away from graduation, Diamond smashed all of her final exams, including her practical exams. She was on her way to a brighter future with less stress and negativity. She remained optimistic despite her troubled marriage. She was determined to make it to the finish line. The only thing left to tackle on her short-term goal list was passing her state final exam to receive her nail tech certification. She had begun earning money doing manicures, pedicures, and acrylic nail enhancements, which made her confidence turn in a positive direction. She had experienced the lowest point in her life, so things could only get better. She believed, achieved, and she RECEIVED!

They Smile in Your Face

It was the last day of class, and Diamond was so proud of her accomplishment. She had applied for graduation and received her invitations. Despite her troubled marriage, she completed her nail tech course and would be graduating with HONORS!

While enjoying the nice spread of food Diamond and her classmates brought to celebrate their accomplishments, Diamond was talking with her classmate, Cookie. Cookie informed Diamond without hesitation of what she heard Tasha telling her sister, Becky. Tasha pretty much had confessed to sleeping with Percy and told Becky how he watched her behind Diamond's back while in the same room. As soon as the words left Cookie's lips, "Tasha is screwing your husband," Diamond felt a weight being lifted off of her shoulders. She explained to Cookie how she had a gut feeling that they had sex one day in particular.

"One night in particular, me and some of my home girls were about to go out to the club. I purposely left Tasha and Percy at me and Keisha's place at the time to go to the store. When Keisha and I returned, my bedroom curtains looked as if they had been pulled down from the window. The rod that held the curtains in place appeared to have been snatched down with force where the nails joined the wall. I was very suspicious. It looked as if they were looking out of the window during the sexual act so that they would see us pull back in the parking lot and not get caught in the act.

"I thought it was very strange that Percy was still there when we returned from the store, and Tasha had not attempted to fry the chicken she was supposed to have been frying during our store run!"

Cookie felt relieved that she was not telling Diamond something that might devastate her but instead confirmed her suspicions.

Diamond later confronted Percy, and, of course, he denied anything happened between them and told Diamond how Tasha came on to him, but he rejected her. Diamond cut Tasha off, and the sisterhood that they once shared would never exist again. Since her marriage was soon ending, she continued her outside relationships and ignored Percy, even though they were back in the same household again.

There were comments made by family members that Diamond should be cutting both Percy and Tasha off and not just Tasha if she felt betrayed by them both. However, Diamond felt the most betrayed by Tasha because some men would be trifling just because they could be.

When you have a sisterhood or BFF, their men are OFF-LIMITS, PERIOD, POINT-BLANK! Whether it's someone from their past, it does not matter. Whether they are separated or divorced, some things you just don't do. But nevertheless, a whore will always be a whore with any man trifling enough to give her the satisfaction!

Well, the apple does not fall far from the tree. Diamond's Aunt Martha, her mom, Honey, and Aunt Glenda had slept with the same men. But at some point, generational curses should be broken and not blamed on drug usage!

Diamond refused to have the same morals and betrayal tactics as her mom and aunts, so she had no other choice but to break the cycle and end the sisterhood with Tasha. Although for the sake of moving on with her life and not harboring bitterness toward them both, she had to forgive them, even though to this day, they still deny that anything happened between them.

Although Diamond had many opportunities to smash a few of Percy's homies, she had more class than that. They were coming at her, left and right, but she was more focused on her future than getting back at Percy. Besides, she was getting her revenge by setting herself up for a successful life without him!

Go Get It

Graduation day had arrived, and Diamond completed one of her short-term goals that would change her life. She was so proud of her accomplishments and the direction her life was headed. Life had begun to have more meaning and purpose. She was looking forward to walking across that victory stage once again!

As Diamond stood in line, awaiting her name to be called by the dean, she could not help but to look back over the past year of her life, how broken and hopeless she felt until she decided to make positive changes in her life. She was so overcome with emotion that tears streamed down her cheeks uncontrollably. She received her certificate of completion, shook the dean's hand, then gave God glory for giving her the endurance to reach the finish line. She was determined to live a purpose-filled life. And from that day forward, she did just that!

Despite his extramarital affairs, Percy was there to support his wife, although Diamond thought at times she would not complete the course due to all of the strife that was going on in her marriage. But against all the odds, SHE DID IT! Percy seemed to be happy for Diamond, even though he added unnecessary drama in her life over the past seven years. She was enjoying her moment. She was in her year of completion and looking forward to the year of new beginnings!

Diamond was still in survival mode although she had completed her nail technician course. She was still hustling to keep her bills paid and awaiting her testing date to take her certification exam, then she would wait another couple of weeks to receive her results.

Percy knew it was just a matter of time that his marriage to Diamond would be over. Little did Diamond know he was plotting to steal her SUV that she had hustled up enough money to purchase as a graduation gift to herself! Percy, for some reason, thought he was entitled to reap the benefits of Diamond's accomplishments. However, God had the final say.

Diamond had been so focused on studying for her certification exam, but she never ceased praying and thanking God for what He was about to do in her life. Percy was still being his selfish self. Nevertheless, Diamond was as unbothered as ever.

She was certain that she would indeed pass her certification exam, so she prepared to move. She moved to an area near the airport, only minutes from the beauty salon where she had been hired to offer nail services.

Diamond's life felt as if she was living and no longer just existing. She woke up each morning with great anticipation as to what would come along with each new day.

Diamond's stomach was filled with nervousness as she awaited her name to be called to enter the testing center. Although she was confident in her skills, she did not know what to expect. What procedures would she be asked to perform? And how critical would the examiners be? Also, what questions would appear on the written portion of the exam?

As she sat there with great anticipation of getting that day behind her, she silently prayed for focus, clarity, and direction as she knew that God was about to do great things in her life. Immediately after Diamond ended her prayer with an amen, her name was called to enter the testing center. She was prepared to ace both the written and the practical portions of the nail tech exam.

Later that day, Diamond signed her rental agreement lease for her new townhome and received her keys. It had to be God that allowed this move to take place, considering she had no proof of income, only her word and bank statement showing only cash deposits. Those deposits were enough to convince the property manager to rent to Diamond. She did not inform the manager of her marriage to Percy. Why bother since they would soon be divorced?

She settled into her new space and continued to hustle funds from her blackjack skills and her gift of gab. Diamond could talk her way into a man's pocket with ease and with a clear conscience.

A couple weeks passed, and she received the letter-sized envelope from the State of Tennessee Cosmetology Board. She opened it up and, in all caps, her test results informed her that she had PASSED her State Board Exam and was officially a certified licensed nail technician.

The next morning, Diamond went to the beauty and barber shop that she had previously spoken with the owners about offering nail services. She was so excited about getting her new career off the ground. They discussed booth rental fees, which she would start out paying a percentage since the salon would be supplying the customers until Diamond could build a regular clientele.

It was June, so business started out steady, which left less time for Diamond to hustle with her side hustle, blackjack. The clientele at the salon was 95 percent Black, which would be a challenge for her to build a consistent flow of repeat business without offering specials and discounts.

Same Mess, Different Day

Percy was up to his same selfish tactics, and his wrongdoings caught up with him. A female that he had been manipulating found out that Percy was married and gave him an ultimatum, insisting that he leave Diamond. The female, we will call Biggum, had been dealing with Percy intimately, which he told Diamond the young lady was a friend's sister that wanted to be more than friends. Biggum apparently caught feelings for a married man and wanted Diamond to know all about their so-called relationship. Biggum crossed the line and somehow found out where Diamond and Percy lived.

She left a note on Diamond's car windshield that pretty much informed Diamond that she and Percy were more than friends. That was the last time Percy would betray her. She had reached her breaking point. She told Percy to get out! He insisted that Biggum was not his latest fling, and to prove it, Diamond asked Percy to file a restraining order. Diamond told Percy, "It was one thing to cheat, but when your actions find their way to our doorstep, you have crossed the line!"

Just in case she tried to harm Diamond in any way, they would have a record on file at the Memphis Police Department restricting Biggum from having contact with them both. Once again, Percy convinced Diamond to let him come back home and insisted that he would be a better husband. For once in his life, he realized that he was about to lose the best blessing God could ever give him, his wife, Diamond. Nothing he said would convince Diamond to continue being his wife. Her mind was made up as they sat in the Domestic Affairs Office, filing an Order of Protection against Biggum.

Diamond had come to the realization that Percy's selfish actions would get her caught up right in the middle of his drama. All Diamond wanted to do was focus on her future, and anything that jeopardized that had to be eliminated, even her husband, Percy.

Percy and Diamond walked out of the courtroom after the hearing of Percy's complaint against Biggum. Although he filed the Order of Protection against Biggum to prove to Diamond he wanted his marriage, it was too late. That situation could have gotten out of hand. If you are going to cheat on your mate, at least cheat with someone that looks better and weighs less than four hundred pounds. That woman was huge, and nine times out of ten, her bankroll was even bigger! She had to be paying Percy to be with her. Diamond felt bad for Biggum. She could only imagine the many lies Percy had told her.

What a day! Diamond was mentally exhausted and needed to release some tension. She knew exactly what she needed and who to get it from. Unfortunately, it would not be Percy. Diamond and Percy left court in separate vehicles as Diamond would not be going straight home for a change. She had to make a detour. Diamond did not care if Percy discovered her infidelity. Besides, she and Percy had not slept together in months. As far as she was concerned, she never wanted to make lust to her soon-to-be estranged husband ever again!

Diamond's Epiphany

Business had started out very slow for Diamond at the salon, and Percy was not much of a provider. Diamond decided that she needed to sell her second vehicle that Percy was using as a means of entertaining his THOTS. Bills needed to be paid, and Percy was not helping lighten Diamond's load. She was not hustling as much because she was at the shop around the clock, trying to build her clientele. She knew that it would be a process, so all she could do was be patient and keep her side pieces that were contributing to her bills.

A couple of months had passed, and Diamond started to feel that void once again. She had not attended church in a while and needed to go and get a word from God. As usual, her church family welcomed her with opened arms. No one asked where she had been or why she had not been to church, which was one of the things she loved about her church. Sometimes, all backsliders need is genuine love and acceptance from their church family.

What an awesome way to start off a week. Church was much needed, and, as usual, it seemed as if Pastor Houston was speaking directly to Diamond. "Two wrongs don't make it right!" As those words rolled off Pastor's tongue, Diamond knew in that moment that she was bound to go to hell! She could see it in her mind, plain as day, Diamond Carter sentenced to spend eternity in hell for giving Percy a taste of his own medicine!

In that moment, the fear of God convicted Diamond in such a way she could never imagine. She was in tears as she asked God to forgive her for cheating on Percy as an act of revenge. And the last encounter would be the last encounter she would have with Bigg Poppa!

Diamond did not even answer his phone calls anymore. She was DONE! Even though Bigg Poppa had plenty of money and the best oral skills on the planet, Diamond had to cut all ties with him IMMEDIATELY!

It was tithes and offering time, and, once again, Diamond was convicted. She and Satan went back and forth as to why she could not pay money that she received from her trick to the church.

She addressed her tithes envelope to pay $60 in tithes to cover the $600 that she had made that week. She did manage to squeeze in a day at the casino when she was off from the salon. The offering plate came around, and she took the envelope out of her purse and put it in the offering plate. Satan told Diamond, "Now you have cursed your damn money, stupid!" Diamond's heart fell to the floor! She wondered if what Satan told her was true.

Several weeks had passed, and business was extremely slow at the shop. Diamond had cut Big Poppa off, and she was on a losing streak at the casino. Diamond could not help but to revisit her mental conversation with Satan. *Damn, was Satan telling me the truth? Did I curse my money?*

The Fourth of July had come and gone. Diamond still was struggling to keep her bills paid. It was July, and Diamond had not even made enough money to pay her rent. She had to make sure she paid her truck note, even if she had to give up her townhome.

Another week ended, and once she paid her booth rent, Diamond barely had $100 to live off for the next week. She contemplated calling Big Poppa, but she removed that thought from her mind. She left the shop that Saturday evening and went home devastated. What was she going to do?

She made it home to find Percy asleep on the couch. She slammed the door to wake his trifling ass up! "What are you doing here, Percy? I thought you were going to be on the road, working for a while."

"Damn, I can't come home to see my beautiful wife?"

"Yeah, if you are paying the rent."

"Diamond, why is the rent not paid?"

"Are you freaking serious, Percy? You know what? I'm good. I'll pay my own damn rent. I've been paying it all this time anyway! Get all of your shit and GET OUT!"

"I'm leaving back out in the morning, Diamond. I was just missing you and wanted to come home and make love to my wife!"

Diamond laughed hysterically. "Are you serious? Percy, my caramel pie wouldn't get wet for you if you were the last man on earth! I won't ever screw your dirty penis tail again!"

"So let me get this straight, the only way you will pay our rent is if I screw you?"

"Like I said, GET ALL OF YOUR SHIT AND DON'T EVER COME BACK HERE AGAIN, PERCY!"

Percy gathered the few clothes he had left there and called someone to pick him up. Diamond took the car key off his key chain while he was in the bathroom. She had planned on changing the door locks ASAP. Once he left, she just sat on the couch, wondering how she was going to pay her rent. She began to cry out to God. "Lord, what am I going to do? Lord, help me, I'm so tired!" She had cried herself to sleep on the couch. Any other Saturday night, Diamond would be partying and hanging out with her associates, but she had given up that lifestyle to focus on her future.

Diamond woke up the next morning with so much peace in her spirit. She turned on the radio to her favorite radio station, 95.7 Hallelujah FM, as she got dressed for church. On the radio came a song that would change her life forever, "Open My Heart" by Yolanda Adams. Diamond stopped getting dressed and sat on the bed, listening to the words of the song. It seemed as if the Holy Spirit had ignited something deep in Diamond's spirit. Diamond did not know what was happening, but her soul settled more at ease each time she heard that song on the radio.

Diamond was ready for church and headed out. She pulled up on the church parking lot, and on came her song again. She closed her eyes, listened, and meditated on the words to the song. The tears just flowed as Diamond sat there and emptied herself from all the years of disappointment, abandonment, betrayal, abuse, depression, three failed suicide attempts, and low self-esteem. God was about to release her from the years of bondage that she had endured. And He would use Yolanda Adam's song to do it!

Diamond got herself together and went inside the church. She was just in time for altar call. She walked up to the altar and began to empty herself once again. She did not realize just how broken she was. She somehow just seemed to manage and deal with the cards that she was dealt called life.

Pastor Houston's morning message was on point as usual. He spoke about God being able to use what we go through to give us a testimony. And, boy, did Diamond have a powerful testimony! That Sunday would be Diamond's first breakthrough. She was well on her way to the healing that she yearned for her entire life.

Betrayed into Purpose

Diamond decided to stay after church to fellowship with a few members, including the first lady of Hope Baptist Church. She expressed to Mrs. Houston how much she would like to get involved with the Praise Dance Ministry. Lady Houston embraced the idea. In fact, she welcomed Diamond with open arms. She informed Diamond when the next rehearsal would be. Diamond was so excited to be Lady Houston's assistant praise dance instructor and Hope Baptist Church's first soloist praise dancer.

A couple weeks passed, and Diamond attended her first dance rehearsal. The Testimonies were rehearsing for an upcoming event. After rehearsal, Diamond expressed to Lady Houston that she would like to perform a solo. The Testimonies would perform an A & B selection, and Diamond would soon discover one of her gifts from God.

Business continued to decrease at the shop, and Diamond's bills were piling up. Diamond decided to sell her second vehicle in order to pay her rent. Almost instantaneously after she parked the vehicle on a vacant lot and placed a For Sale sign inside the window, someone stopped by to inquire about it. The next day, Diamond would have her rent paid, and she did not have to sleep with anyone, hustle at the casino, or rely on Big Poppa for it.

Diamond was new to discovering what having faith was all about. She prayed and asked God to make a way for her to get her rent paid without manipulating a man to get it done. And He did just that. Diamond met with the buyer of her second car, signed over the title, and walked away with her rent and grocery money!

Several more weeks passed, and business continued to be slow, but Diamond kept her word to Lady Houston. Their performance was approaching, and Diamond was not allowing her financial circumstances to keep her from fulfilling what the Holy Spirit placed on her heart. The final rehearsal had been completed. Diamond and the Testimonies were scheduled to perform Sunday. Diamond never rehearsed; she was going to allow the Holy Spirit to lead her movements.

After a very discouraging week at the salon, Diamond settled her booth rent with Mrs. Mary, the salon owner, and ended her workweek. She had to leave the salon earlier than usual to go purchase her dance attire and ballet shoes for tomorrow's performance. She left the salon, made it to the parking lot where her truck was parked, and discovered it had been stolen! She furiously called the police to report it stolen. Then she called Lady Houston to inform her that she would not be able to perform.

Lady Houston told Diamond that Satan wanted her to walk away from her breakthrough. God wanted to use her, and she impeccably had to go through trials to get the blessing God had in store for her life. Lady Houston called Diamond's cousin Charles to see if he could help. Charles picked Diamond up from the salon, and they went to purchase Diamond's dance attire. Diamond was so distraught, wondering why someone would steal her truck!

Diamond did not make much money again that week, but she did have enough to invest in her gift. They made it to the dance attire store right before they closed. Charles also told Diamond that Satan wanted her to quit, and she could not give him the satisfaction. Charles took Diamond home and offered to pick her up for church the next morning and then to the banquet hall where the program was being held.

Sunday morning was not the usual Sunday morning. Diamond was without transportation, but she had so much peace in her spirit and joy in her heart. Diamond received a call from the police department stating that they located her truck in Texas. "Texas!" Diamond replied, "Well, whoever has it, I want to press charges!"

"Well, ma'am, the man that has it says that he's your husband, and by law, we can't arrest him because your truck is conjugal property."

"Sir, we are separated, and Percy does not even have keys to my truck!"

"Yes, ma'am, he stated that you all had an argument about the keys, so he got the extra set from the dealership! So, as I stated, we can't arrest him for auto theft. You may want to contact him and ask him to return your truck, ma'am. We will be closing this case as the vehicle has been located. I am sorry, ma'am, but it's the law." Diamond hung up the phone in total disbelief as to what the officer told her.

Diamond called her cousin Charles and told him not to pick her up for church. Percy had stolen her truck and basically, by law, got away with it! Charles informed Diamond to go ahead and get dressed for church because he was picking her up for church. "Diamond, you can't let Satan be a distraction from getting a word from God. I'll be there in about an hour!"

They arrived at church just in time for Pastor Houston's morning message, titled "It's Only a Test!" Those words pierced Diamond's heart to the core. She kept repeating that phrase, "It's only a test." Although she was furious about Percy stealing her only means of transportation that he did not put a dime on, she took the pastor's message at heart. And, boy, was she being tested in a major way!

After service, Lady Houston asked Diamond how she was doing and reassured her that God is in control, and He would return her truck. She wanted Diamond to stay focused on her performance so that the Holy Spirit could use her that afternoon. In spite of Diamond's frustration, Diamond needed to hear Lady Houston's words of comfort. The thought of God using her did something to her spirit that she had never experienced before.

Later that Sunday afternoon, Charles and Diamond arrived at the banquet hall. They were greeted by Lady Houston with the biggest smile on her face as if she had a conversation with God and knew what the outcome of Diamond's performance would be. Lady Houston and one of the Testimonies' moms assisted Diamond with her attire as the program was getting started. The welcome was done, the devotion, and then it was time for Diamond to take the stage.

The prayer that Lady Houston prayed was still in Diamond's spirit as the music started to play. Diamond's spirit vacated her body as the Holy Spirit filled her temple. Her unrehearsed performance received a standing ovation! And for the first time in her life, she could feel the love of God on her life. She knew that everything that she had endured throughout her life led to that moment!

A Word of Encouragement from the Author

On this journey we call life, we will be faced with trials and tribulations. We will be discouraged, and we will deal with fear at times. But always remember God placed something unique inside of each one of us. We must follow our hearts and act upon that thing that makes us tingle inside, that undeniable thing that makes us feel good inside. Whatever passion lies inside of you, don't ignore it! Pursue it, eat, sleep, and breathe it! Use it to bless others!

God gave it to YOU, and no one else can bring it to pass but YOU! Even when people laugh at your ideas, STICK TO IT! That feeling will not go away! Encourage yourself. Even when other people don't cheer for you, cheer for YOURSELF! The worst thing you can do is deny yourself from operating in your gift or gifts! God gave it to you for a purpose, and only you can fulfill it! Not Mom, Dad, your kids, your spouse—only YOU!

What are you waiting for? The world needs your gift. Please don't be selfish with it. God wants to bless you in a mighty way! And what's so awesome about it? It will take very little effort because God has perfected it! But you will have to put in the work of it being flawless. And, yes, He wants to use you too, even you!

If I did not seek the Lord, I would still be in the bondage of low self-esteem, depression, and succeeded at suicide because of hurtful words spoken to me by someone that did not love himself and did not know God. Never accept being treated less than you deserve, but first KNOW that you are a king or queen, and they don't deserve you!

He has equipped you with the tools you need, and, yes, He will provide the resources for you to do what he called you to do! I can't wait to see you at the finish line! BE BLESSED!

Acknowledgments

Thank you, Lord and Savior, Jesus Christ. I am NOTHING without you! Thank you for loving me, flaws and all! Continue to use me in a mighty way to fulfill your purpose for my life that you get the glory!

Thanks to my parents, William E. Hughey Jr. (In Loving Memory) and Estella Anthony, for creating such an amazing human being! Love you both with every fiber in me! Forgive me for the explicit language, not too much, but you both know how I love to verbally express myself.

Special thanks to my sister and my lifetime supporter, Delilah Hughey Ellis. Thank you for always believing in me mostly when I did not believe in myself. I love you so much!

And last but certainly not least, special thanks to everyone that took my love and pure heart for granted. Thank God for giving me the gift of discernment and allowing me to recognize when a person has fulfilled their purpose in my life. If we crossed paths at some point and no longer rock together, THANK YOU for propelling me to my destiny! From the bottom of my heart, I forgive you, and may God fill you with whatever you lack from having a pure heart as well. Again, thank you and God bless!

For I know the plans I have for you, declares
the Lord, plans to prosper you and not to harm
you, plans to give you hope and a future.

—Jeremiah 29:11

About the Author

Evangelist Sherida Hughey is a native California girl by way of Memphis, Tennessee. She currently resides in the mid-South, where she founded and operates a nonprofit organization, Gyft of Gaab Ministries. GGM was established on the principles of assisting lost souls to find purpose in their lives through sharing life experiences, teaching the Word of God, mentoring, motivational speaking, life/spiritual coaching, and laughter therapy in the form of Christian comedy.

GGM specializes in the areas of abandonment, self-esteem, domestic violence counseling, prison ministry, drug/alcohol abuse recovery, depression, and much more! Visit us at gyftofgaabministries.com or via Facebook—Evangelist Sherida Hughey or Gyft of Gaab Ministries Page. You may also sow a seed to GGM via Cash App $GGM4GOD. All proceeds and donations are distributed accordingly.

www.ingramcontent.com/pod-product-compliance
Lightning Source LLC
Chambersburg PA
CBHW022119150726

47990CB00003B/1427